# Dandy Lions and Dandelions



Sally Young

BookLeaf Publishing

Presentation by *BookLeaf Publishing*

Web: www.bookleafpub.com

E-mail: info@bookleafpub.com

ISBN: 9789357443180

First edition 2023

*I'd like to dedicate this book to my family - love you all x*

# ACKNOWLEDGEMENT

I'd like to thank my family and friends for being behind me and supporting me in writing my poems.

# PREFACE

I've always enjoyed writing poems. I enjoy writing about people I know and I like my poems to rhyme.

This book is a collection of poems of different topics for the young and older readers. I hope you enjoy reading them as much as I did writing them.

# Happy Together

They met through their jobs
When she needed a lift
He arrived in his Taxi
In the back she did sit

They chatted, they laughed
Jokes they would tell
It was clear from day one
That they got on so well

It was a good time later
That their feelings arose
And one sunny day
How they felt was disclosed

It wasn't easy at first
They had ups, they had downs
They had smiles, they had laughter
They had tears, they had frowns

But together they stayed
And grew stronger and stronger
And the love they shared
Grew bigger and longer

Then just before Christmas
He got down on one knee
With tears in his eyes
He said, "please marry me"?

She said yes straight away
Her smile was so big
And they both started looking
For a place for their shindig

Honeymoon was booked
They ordered the flowers
Dresses were altered
The favours took hours

But the stresses and planning
It had all been worthwhile
As his face lit up
As she walked up the aisle

So as the bride and groom
Start their new life
Let's toast the new husband
And his beautiful wife

# Clowning Around

I went to the circus
And saw lots of clowns
Some of them had great big smiles
And some of them had frowns

Some of them had orange hair
That looked like bits of wool
All of them were brightly dressed
None of them were dull

Some of them were wearing shirts
Covered in bright spots
Others had on trousers
In yellow polka dots

One was wearing great big shoes
Which made his feet look big
And one he rode a unicycle
Whilst others danced a jig

When the show was over
I waved to say goodbye
And from the circus ring was thrown
A great big custard pie

# A winter walk

I took a walk on a winters day
The snow crunching beneath my feet
Perfect footprints left behind
All pristine and neat

The air was cold, the sky was blue
I could see my breath in the air
The winter flowers bowed their heads
And the trees were all so bare

The park looked so pretty
All glistening and white
The snow and frost were twinkling
Beneath the winter sunlight

The ducks were huddled together
In the reeds by the frozen lake
Whilst children playing nearby
Were catching falling snowflakes

The winter days are pretty
But soon it will be spring
Flower shoots will start to show
And new nestlings will start to sing

# Grandpa

When I was a little girl
I'd sit on Grandpa's knee
He'd tell me about when he was young
Whilst sipping on his tea

He walked three miles to school each day
Often on his own
Winter mornings were cold and dark
But he walked it without a groan

He'd tell me about his friends
And the things they liked to play
Hide and seek, cards or jacks
To pass the time away

His clothes were often hand me downs
From his cousin, which was kind
Often they had holes in
But Grandpa didn't mind

Grandpa said the times were hard
But he always felt so blessed
He wouldn't change a single thing
They simply were the best

# Blue

Blue is how you sometimes feel
When your day just isn't right
Blue is the colour of the sky
On a day that's shining bright

Blue is the colour of bluebells
As they shoot up in the spring
Blue is the olive wing butterfly
With its colourful, dainty wing

Blue is the colour of peacocks
Its feathers with coloured blue spots
Blue is a promise you can give
With a bloom of forget - me - nots

# Dandy Lion and Dandelion

The Lion is all fine and dandy
With his hair of gold
He's known to be the jungle king
He's fierce, he's big, he's bold

The dandelion with its golden head
Is king of the village flowers
After the harsh cold winter
It displays its strength and powers

The dandy Lion and dandelion
In some ways are the same
They're hardy, strong and tough
And they share a golden mane

# Christmas

Christmas time is coming
And Santa's on his way
With Rudolph as his reindeer
And presents on his sleigh

He's all dressed up in red and white
With a hat upon his head
And presents around the tree he'll leave
Whilst you're all tucked up in bed

But don't forget to leave
A carrot and mince pie
For Santa and his reindeer
Before they wave goodbye

# The Owl

When all the children are in bed
And the stars are shining bright
The wide eyed owl wakes up from sleep
And hunts for food all night

And when he's finished hunting
Had all he wants for tea
He makes his noise tu-whit tu-whoo
Whilst sitting in his tree

And when the morning sun
Comes to brighten up the day
The wide eyed owl goes back to sleep
So that you and me can play

# My Friend

My friend is there to pick me up
On days that I feel blue
He always has the right words
And knows what I've been through

My friend is there when I need a chat
And we'll have a cup of tea
He's there with an ear to listen
And he's always there for me

My friend is there for giggles
We laugh until we cry
We go on trips, we wine and dine
On him I can rely

My friend he is my husband
And I love him with all my heart
I'll always be there for him
Even on days we're apart

# Have You Ever Wondered?

Have you ever wondered why
A flamingo is so pink
Or why a skunk so beautiful
Let's off an awful stink

Have you ever wondered why
A camel has a hump
Why many of our animals leap
But elephants can't jump

Have you ever wondered
If penguins have knees
Why do crabs walk sideways
And why can sharks not sneeze

Have you ever wondered why
The Lion's the jungle king
Or why monkeys jump from tree to tree
And use their tales to swing

These animals make us wonder
From the slippery to the sleek
To the tiny, to the tall
They're all different and unique

# Spring

Bee's buzzing, butterflies fluttering
Lambs bleating as they're born
Mornings are crisp, days are brighter
Buttercups cover the lawn

Easter time, children laughing
Hunting for eggs and treats
Cups of tea, hot cross buns
Toasted, buttered and sweet

Bunnies hopping, chick's chirping
Birds wake us as they sing
Snowdrops, bluebells, daffodils
These are signs of spring

# The Seaside

A day at the seaside
Is my favourite place to be
Digging, making sandcastles
And paddling in the sea

I watch the crabs walk sideways
Snapping with their claws
I like to save the starfish
That are stranded on the shore

The shells they look like treasure
All across the sand
And clumps of shredded seaweed gather
Where the water meets the land

I like to stay at the seaside
Until the end of day
And watch the glowing sun
As it lowers across the bay

# Halloween

There's a ghost at the window
And vampires at the door
There's a grave stone in the garden
And a goblin with one claw

There's children all dressed up
Playing trick or treat
Carrying little cauldrons
Filled with candy sweets

If you look into the sky
You'll see the swooping bats
There's witches on broomsticks
Along with their cats

There's pumpkins outside houses
All with a scary face
There's skeletons in hiding
Let's hope they don't give chase

Halloween can be scary
But it's also lots of fun
There's apple bobbing games to play
When the outdoor time is done

# Autumn

The leaves are changing colour
To red, brown and gold
And as the nights draw in
It's beginning to feel cold

Cosy nights by the fire
So warm, it feels nice
Drinking hot chocolate
Flavoured with pumpkin spice

Conkers begin to fall
From the swaying tree
The wind gently blows them
Until they are free

Squirrels collect acorns
To hide in the ground
And once they finish digging
They scurry around

In the middle of the field
The proud scarecrow stands
With a hat upon his head
And straw for his hands

Hats, scarves and gloves are worn
As the weather becomes duller
But Autumn is so pretty
With its ever changing colour

# Differently Able

People always look
People always stare
But what are they looking at?
It's only a wheelchair

My legs may not work
And I may bump the table
There's no need to stare at me
I'm just differently able

I may be in a wheelchair
I may not be the same
As you or any other
But please don't show me shame

I fight against the odds
Almost every day
And although there's things I cannot do
I'm unique in my own way

# Not Just a Carer

I wake her up
I get her dressed
I brush her hair
To look her best

I clean her teeth
Put on her coat
I brush her hair
On her I dote

We go for lunch
We like to drink tea
She likes funny noises
Made by me

We go to the park
We walk for miles
We often hug
She gives me smiles

We play with her toys
She loves her bells
She often laughs
She sometimes yells

If she's unhappy
To her I'll tend
I'm not just her carer
I'm also her friend

# I Love to Dance

I love to dance
And move my feet
I dance to old music
I dance in the street

I like to do the Samba
I love to do the Swing
I can't go on my tip toe
So Ballets not my thing

I love to dance the night away
I like to do the bop
The Cha cha's not my favourite
But I like to do hip hop

I think Flamenco looks pretty
And Ballroom's really classy
And when I do the fox trot
I like to think I'm sassy

# The Sky at Night

Do you ever wonder
When you look up at the sky
Who else is there looking
At the stars way up high

Do they look up at the moon
Can they see its grey and white
Do they wonder too
Why it shines so bright

I'd love to see a spaceman
In a spacecraft of blue
I wonder if other people
Would like to see that too

Did they see the shooting star
As it flew from outer space
Did it make them look in wonder
Was there a smile on their face

www.ingramcontent.com/pod-product-compliance
Lightning Source LLC
Chambersburg PA
CBHW051717130826
49812CB00034B/1222
*9789357443180*